The Concrete Window

Safa Ali

BookLeaf Publishing

Presentation by *BookLeaf Publishing*

Web: www.bookleafpub.com

E-mail: info@bookleafpub.com

ISBN: 9789357697163

First edition 2023

DEDICATION

For the people that find beauty in ugly times.

ACKNOWLEDGEMENT

My first debt is to my mother who showed the upmost strength and resilience throughout my childhood. She showed me what it is to be an intelligent woman and presented vehemence in her solidarity. Watching her model a type of motherhood that took many sacrifices from her, taught me that the beauty of womanhood is in being nurturing and exhibiting kindness, even against all opposition and despotism. She was not only my mother, but my friend, and I can only hope that she holds me as hers. i'm

I would like to thank my best friend, Maryam, for being an ear to my woes, and for reading my insufferable and pretentious writing during my early stages. Her support was unwavering and she never once let me lose hope for a successful and independent future. Without her motivation I would have been completely alone at times. without her, i would have given up faith for healing and happiness long ago.
i would like to thank my childhood best friend, Khadija, who hasn't moved from my side since i met her when we were 12. She has been a safe haven for me, she feels like home and without her by my side during my youth, I wouldn't be

the woman I am today. She gave me guidance and encouragement and I can never put into words the love I feel for her.
For both of you, it's more than a friendship, but a sisterhood.

Finally, but not least of all in importance, I would like to thank myself for being my own biggest supporter, partner and friend when it felt like I had no one. I gave my blood, sweat and tears for this and I bought woke up after nights of crying myself to sleep and made sure I worked hard still. I persisted and I did it alone for the most part and for that, I am grateful to myself, someone who I rarely remember to give thanks to and show my appreciation for. I carried on aiming for the stars even when people told me that a woman like me couldn't be a writer or an artist, but here I am, thanks to my own perseverance.

the pen

on some days I awake to find myself unable to live
with the fact of existence and the pain of it's
symptoms.
days when I express myself through yawning and
picking at the cracks in my lips.
days when words seem futile and working seems
ineffectual.
days when my hunger satisfies itself and lust, for life,
for people, for being, is sated by emptiness.

on those days, I will write.

when all else fails me, my pen will not.
this is the virtue of the pen, for my mind is a mess
and my pen will detangle it and turn it into something
wonderful, it will find beauty in ugly times.

clumsy words

I speak to her sometimes,
she nods but I am not sure if she listens.

I speak to her in clumsy words,
mother tongue, fading from memory.

I speak to her boldly, in colours and shapes,
which only receives reprimand.

I speak to her from the deepest depths of my sorrow,
it only elicits a "try not to think about it"

so I try not to think about it.
but every night I find myself speaking to her.

silence screams

she sits opposite me at the kitchen table stirring her tea with shaky hands. she doesn't need to say anything, I can feel her hurt from here. even after all those years she still feels the shadow of her beaten down spirit from that old house, chasing her now around ours. It eats at her while she starves herself to fit into the crevice of some arm. she is silent but so loud. it's hard to ignore her screaming trauma.

how were you so old at only 16? you were so young when you behaved 35 and now you cry like an overgrown child.

you can put your strength down now, it's safe here. you don't need to say anything, just sit. let me butter your toast and stir your tea, let me feed you with my hands. if I could, I would have all those years ago, but i'm here now.

teeth

the earth has chewed me up and spit me out more times than i can count. for so long i came back each time and made myself softer, easier to chew, easier to swallow, easier to digest. so soft, so small that i could become nothing inside of it. i wasted so many of my years trying to become softer for the earth but all along it was the earth that didn't have the teeth for me.

ode to fear

I have always wondered why I cry so easily,
why the weight of existence seems so heavy, and
why the tears explode from my eyes.
but the more tears I bled, the more I realised that
I come from a long line of women who
swallowed their tears,
and devoured their pain,
who went about their life as if the sadness was
an expected part of womanhood.
so I cry for my mother and my aunts and their
mothers before them,
who bred their pain into me.
I cry for their bruises and their scars,
for their calloused hands and overworked knees,
for the dreams that were snatched from them
before they reached womanhood,
for the fear that I will be just like them.

mellowing out my mind

some mornings I and find myself unable to leave my bed.
I try to lift myself up but my limbs pull me back into the familiar safety of my bedsheets.
the world is too cold for me.
so, I listen to music and watch the gaps of sunlight dance in the trees.
I make tea because it will warm my hands in the way that I wish someone else could.
I make an attempt to clean my room by hiding messes in cramped drawers.
and maybe after I'm done distracting my mind from the obsessive anxieties, I'll go back and collapse in fear, but at least ill have my music and my tea and my tidy room, and for a moment life will be bearable.

when grief knocks at your door

you have to be careful when grief knocks at you door,
for it is known to be rather discourteous visitor.
let it in for too long,
and you may find that it has made itself welcome
without invitation.
before long, your shelves are empty,
your favourite fruits have been eaten,
you'll be hungry with nothing to eat.
grief makes a home in the body,
and it sleeps in your veins,
it occupies a new room each night,
it hollows out each new cavity,
and fills it with a new fear,
so be careful when grief knocks at your door,
and be sure to get rid of it before it evicts you.

girlhood

I sweeten my voice with sugar free tea,
I widen my eyes,
I feign naivety.

I hide my anger
and bite my tongue till it bleeds,
because a good girl doesn't put up a fight.

my blood runs cherry red,
lick it up, it's sweet like me.

gorgon slain

they called her a monster, medusa, but I still don't know how. for she was raped for her beauty and murdered for her ugliness. they made a bloodbath of her body, so she made one of theirs. and women hunt witches too, because the goddesses made a gorgon of her. punished for a gods crime, isn't that the essence of girlhood? fighting a man who thinks himself a god, only for your defence to become the offence.

the beast of hunger

what will I write about in ten years when the
hunger stops?
now,
I sit on my window sill
and drink
chamomile tea.
now,
I lay in bed
with my notebook in hand
conjuring up
pretty words for ugly days.
now,
I call a friend
and tell them I'm starving.
the hunger will stop though.
one day.
and what will I do then?
because now,
I fear my hunger has become my muse.

homesick

"I want to go home," I think to myself, often while I'm lying in my own bed. I've been trying to go home my whole life. I haven't found it yet. I suffer from these intense spells of homesickness as I sit in my bedroom. I'm not really thinking of a place, but I like to imagine that home feels like when everything is finally over, when you can rest. I imagine a cinnamon candle burning while an apple pie is in the oven. I imagine the feeling when you lie to the school nurse about feeling unwell for someone to pick you up. I imagine telling someone to come and sit at the table with me before the tea gets cold. I imagine home an awful lot but I don't know where it is. I've been trying to home my whole life.

a shot to the heart

she has a crimson scar
on her chest from a bullet wound.
I asked her what being shot in the heart feels like
and she told me that
"some wounds speak for themselves".

to define force

daughterhood was a strange thing for me. strange for my soul to be so constrained. the soul isn't born to be a victim of constraint. strange for my heart to not know where it belongs. I was not supposed to be nobody's daughter. I was not supposed to live with a begging to belong. strange for my mind to be forced into stillness. a still mind will become a dead mind. and a dead mind will eventually take the life from your heart in attempt to regain its livelihood. yes, daughterhood was a strange thing for me, for my soul, heart and mind were ripped from me and I became a thing. I died a small death and I bought myself back and I killed myself so many times but daughterhood is a strange thing and each time I came back to fight it with all I had left.

the orange

let us stand in the dim kitchen lights
and peel an orange.
come stand behind me,
let me peel it and
get the citrus under my nails.
let it sting the paper cut on my fingertips.
let me peel the slices away and place them in
your hand,
let our fingers brush and
let the juice leak from finger to hand to wrist.
let me share my orange with you.

springs child

she was springs child,
born and reborn again.
chewed up and spat out,
she raised herself.

took with her the myths and fables,
took with her l'histoire de mes folies,
they were etched into her bone,
engraved on her heart.

she was springs child,
she planted poppy fields
and sang a solemn prayer,
she raised herself.

twin flame

outside of my window,
the war waged on.
outside was arson smoke,
and battle cries of muscle-clad monsters.

inside of my chambers,
the hearth was warming.
I came back to it each time,
and in it, my flickering love light.

inside of my chambers,
respite from the push-and-shoving,
a flame that burnt so bright it blinded me,
and in doing so, i stopped seeing the war outside.

the sadist's song

he sits at his armchair,
cigar in hand,
puffing out smoke.
this air
is so thick
and so murderous.
it stings my eyes,
it's heavy and hot.
my breath is slow
and straggling,
my lungs are heaving,
his smoke is
all-consuming.
it fills the room,
it's all grey now,
he watches silently
while the smoke
strangles me.
he asks me,
"does it hurt?"
I say "yes".
he says "sorry,"
and lights up another.

eternity and a day

when they ask me what it is that stops my blood, I am afraid I have no answer.
it isn't a thing.

it is painful enough for me to scream until my blood thickens.
it is hollow enough for me to stare at the ceiling in numbness.

it is the days when I scroll mindlessly.
it is never being fully asleep or fully awake.

it is cold hands and thin hair.
it is my body starved and my mind bloated.

it is grey skin under the bronzed powder.
it is bitten lips in designer.

it is "I'm not hungry", while my stomach turns.
it is a distorted mirror and a screaming reflection.

it is a screaming loneliness worsened by my own seclusion.
it is a fear to leave my room for the war that has been invited outside.

it is the empty document that stares at me while my mind paces.

it is the book begging for my attention while I stare absentmindedly.

it is the angry man in your house, and the angrier one you're about to let in.
it is the broken woman beaten and bruised.

it is so many things.
but if you ask me what it is,
I am afraid I have no answer.

sound and sin

a hasty
a hasty but raging
a hasty but raging moment,
when the crime matched the punishment.

a long line

I have always wondered why I cry so easily,
why the weight of existence seems so heavy, and why
the tears explode from my eyes.
but the more tears I bled, the more I realised that I
come from a long line of women who swallowed
their tears,
and devoured their pain,
who went about their life as if the sadness was an
expected part of womanhood.
so I cry for my mother and my aunts and their
mothers before them,
who bred their pain into me.
I cry for their bruises and their scars,
for their calloused hands and overworked knees,
for the dreams that were snatched from them before
they reached womanhood,
for the fear that I will be just like them.

letter to myself

your heart will only break as many times as you let it. it can be put together just as many times as it was pulled apart.

your mind will heal and regain its strength. it will grow when you read again, it will dance on the pages and sing the words to you.

your family are only your family until one of you washes the blood from your hands. your knuckles will only be bruised until you turn away.

one day you'll listen to a sad song on the bus and it will play the sound of an old film you've seen. you'll think to yourself "maybe things aren't so bad".

your hands will only be as cold as the house you live in. one day you'll sit by a warm fireplace with clammy hands and a racing heart.

www.ingramcontent.com/pod-product-compliance
Lightning Source LLC
Chambersburg PA
CBHW062205160726
48282CB00027B/1004
* 9 7 8 9 3 5 7 6 9 7 1 6 3 *